Women of Valor:
Journaling Through the Women of the Bible

A Seasons Illustrated Bible Journaling Study

by

Sara Laughed

To Kate:
Woman of Valor, Sister in Christ.

"Strength and dignity are her clothing,
and she laughs at the time to come.
She opens her mouth with wisdom,
And the teaching of kindness is on her tongue."
Proverbs 31:25-26

TABLE OF CONTENTS

Genesis (handwritten, vertical, beside chapters 5–9)

I.
GUIDE TO THIS STUDY

1

ABOUT THIS STUDY

Welcome to the Women of Valor study! We are so excited to have you with us. *Women of Valor: Journaling Through the Women of the Bible* is designed to be a twelve-week Bible journaling challenge and Bible study. Bible journaling is a form of devotional art, in which people make art in the margins or pages of their Bibles, or in separate notebooks if they're so inclined. Often, this artwork is shared online in communities on Facebook, via blogs, or through other media. Seasons Illustrated, which writes and hosts Women of Valor, has its own Facebook community, called Seasons Illustrated Bible Journaling. Please join us!

This guide is broken up into two parts. Part One, which includes an introduction, some information on Bible journaling, and a basic supply list, will help you get acquainted with Bible journaling. Part Two contains the body of this study, digging into the stories of twelve women of the Bible. Each woman's story includes the primary verses about that woman, a summary of her story, and questions for contemplation and reflection, as well as a Bible journaling prompt. Please make sure that you read the Biblical text as well as the summaries in these chapters! While I do my best to make the summaries accurate and accessible, the Bible itself holds so much more richness than I could ever convey.

This study includes free access to a series of printables and journaling inserts that you can choose to use as you get used to the process of Bible journaling. You can access these printables, as well as a selection of Bible verse prints, at the Seasons Illustrated resource library (http://seasonsillustrated.com/free-library). The password is:

psalm16:8

exactly as shown, without periods, spaces, or capital letters. Enjoy!

2

BIBLE JOURNALING FOR BEGINNERS

This Bible study is unique to other studies because it engages in the devotional practice of Bible journaling. Many people participating are excited to begin Bible journaling, but don't know where to start. I know that taking notes in your Bible can be a little intimidating, let alone drawing, lettering, and painting in it! For that reason, this chapter will be a brief guide on how to get started in your journaling Bible for those of you who haven't yet.

Understanding what it's all about

Bible journaling is not about making the most beautiful art. I, myself, am guilty of wanting to make something really beautiful and impressive for the sake of, well... making something really beautiful and impressive! But that attitude isn't as fulfilling and meaningful as one that dwells in practice. Journaling isn't about the outcome, it's about the process. Focus on connecting with what you're doing, and the skill will come with time.

Finding a verse

You have your Bible, your pen(s), and maybe some extras, like paints, stamps, or stickers. (If you don't yet, check out a few recommendations in the next chapter!) The next thing to do is find a verse.

Bible journaling can be a little scary, especially if you're not used to writing in your Bible. I recommend starting off with a verse that you know well and that means a lot to you. Beginning with a verse that you are familiar with helps take away some level of discomfort when it comes to journaling in your Bible for the first time, and it may spark an idea faster. But choose a verse you know and like before journaling your favorite verse. If you choose your absolute favorite, it may be difficult to come up with a design that includes everything it means to you. Start small until you're comfortable.

Getting inspired

I'm a creative soul, but I'm not an artistic soul. I find

it difficult to come up with entirely new designs for things. I like to find inspiration – and with the internet, that's easier to do now than ever.

You can use Pinterest to browse designs that inspire you, or you can join a Bible journaling group on Facebook, such as our group, Seasons Illustrated Bible Journaling. You can also do a Google search for "Bible journaling" and the verse you chose, to see designs that other people have done with that same verse! Finding inspiration in places like these is a great way to get started with Bible journaling and figure out your style and the kinds of art you'd like to try.

Getting started

Now comes the exciting part! Once you have your tools and verse, it's time to get started. Everyone has a different process for how they do this; for me, it helps to begin in prayer. In the end, what it comes down to is mustering up the courage to put pen to paper and make something that expresses how you feel.

This is my method for the actual journaling process:

1. *Reflect on the verse.* Read it over a few times; maybe do a little background reading. Let it sink into your bones. I think about the parts of the verse that mean something to me, and then I try to figure out how I can represent them in art.

2. *Sketch it out with a pencil.* I like to use a simple mechanical pencil to do my sketching so that I don't make any permanent mistakes!

3. *Outline it with pen.* I use my skinny Pigma Microns to do this, as they don't bleed through the paper. You can read about them in the next chapter.

4. *Fill it in with color.* Next, I use gel pens, colored pencils, and watercolor pencils to add color and dimension to my design.

That's it! Everyone's process is different, but starting with a small and simple design may be helpful if you haven't journaled before. Once you get more comfortable with Bible journaling, you can go ahead and experiment with paints, stamps, and stickers. The Word is your canvas!

3

BASIC SUPPLIES FOR BIBLE JOURNALING

I'll start by saying that you need absolutely nothing to do Bible journaling other than a Bible and a pen. Really. You may have seen people with beautiful paints, stamps, and tabs in their Bibles, but all of those people got started with what you probably already have in your house.

That said, if you'd like to buy a special journaling Bible or you would like to invest in pens that don't bleed through thin paper, I have some recommendations.

Favorite Bible: Black ESV Single Column Journaling Bible by Crossway

Crossway has a very beautiful selection of Bibles that are specifically intended for Bible journaling. The two that I use, shown in the photos throughout this book, are two editions of the ESV single column journaling Bible. I love that this Bible opens flat, whether you're flipping open to Genesis or Revelation. I also really love the cream-colored paper and the size and font of the text.

Favorite pens: Sakura Pigma Micron 01 Ink Pen Set

Having used gel pens, rollerballs, and a variety of other pens on Bible paper, I can say that bleed-through is a huge problem. It's frustrating and it makes the other side of the paper harder to read. Pigma Micron pens are designed for archival paper, so the ink does not bleed through, even on very thin paper like that found in most Bibles. The tips are very fine, so it is easy to take small notes in the margins, or make bigger doodles.

Favorite highlighters: Zebra Eco Zebrite Double-Ended Highlighters

When it comes to liquid highlighters, these are my favorite for Bible journaling by far. They go on smoothly and don't bleed through the paper. I use the fine-tip highlighters so I can highlight line by line if I want to. As with the Pigma Micron pens, these highlighters "ghost" through the paper a little, meaning you can see a touch of color on the other side — but there is no bleed through, and the ghosting is less than I have had with any other product.

Other products

In addition to these products, I use colored pencils, watercolor pencils, washi tape, and other products. Many other people use stamps and stickers — it's all up to you! Go through your house or your local craft store and find the things that inspire you. Good luck and have fun!

II.
WOMEN OF VALOR

4

INTRODUCTION

Sarah. Rachel. Elizabeth. Mary. These names conjure within us images of strong, resilient, and fundamentally human women. They may be the names of our mothers, our daughters, or ourselves. But they are also the names of our spiritual ancestors; the women who came before us, who left us a legacy to uphold or reject.

Their names are woven through our scriptures like threads in a tapestry; not making up the whole design, but contributing to its richness and intricacy. We trace our fingers along their strands, watching as the twists and turns of a single life can change the course of history. As imperfectly human as they were, God used them in the unfolding of one of the greatest stories ever told: that of a people created, fallen, and redeemed.

But these women are important not just because of the roles they play within the greater stories of the Bible. They are also important because they give us a glimpse into ourselves. We relate to them, learn from them, and are reminded through their stories that, just as God used, loved, and redeemed these women, so God uses, loves, and redeems us.

In this twelve-week Bible journaling challenge, we encourage you to join us in reading and journaling the stories of twelve women of the Bible: Hagar, Sarah, Rebecca, Leah, Rachel, Miriam, Ruth, Hannah, Elizabeth, Mary of Nazareth, Mary Magdalene, and Phoebe. At their worst, these women can remind us of the very lowest ways people can behave. But at their best, they bring to mind the praises sung of the nameless woman in Proverbs 31, the eshet chayil: a wife of noble character, a woman of worth, a woman of valor.

Together as we journal the women of the Bible, we will discover what it means to be a woman of valor. Laugh with Sarah and we experience her doubt and wonder. Pray with Hannah as we witness her grief and faithfulness. Sing with Mary as we experience her immense awe and joy at the glory of God.

5

HAGAR

This week's reading: Genesis 16; Genesis 21:8-21

This week's journaling focus: Genesis 16:7-13

It may be unexpected to begin a study of women of the Bible with Hagar. After all, Hagar isn't a matriarch, like Sarah. She isn't the subject of her own story, like Ruth. She isn't even a free woman; instead, she is a Sarah's servant and Abraham's concubine. Hagar's secondary status is woven into her very name: depending on who you ask, it may mean flight, foreigner, or stranger. But despite her earthly status and the fact that she is seen as 'less-than' in the eyes of man, God sees her, and Hagar, not once, but twice, receives something that few other women in the Bible do: a revelation from God.

Hagar's Story

Part One: Hagar in Captivity

We meet Hagar in Genesis 16. Sarah, Abraham's wife, had has wanted a child for years; when she cannot conceive, she brings Hagar to Abraham to serve as a surrogate. In order for Hagar to offer Abraham a legitimate heir, she had to become Abraham's second wife (Genesis 16:3), putting Sarah in what was surely an emotionally challenging position: the woman who could offer Abraham what he and Sarah so desperately wanted would now be elevated from concubine to a similar position to that which Sarah herself had with Abraham. When Hagar indeed becomes pregnant, she "looked with contempt on her mistress" (Genesis 16:4). Sarah, maybe affected by hurt or jealousy, becomes furious and "dealt harshly" (Genesis 16:6) with Hagar. Though the Bible doesn't tell us what she does, we know that it is enough to push Hagar to run into the wilderness, trying, it seems, to find her way back to Egypt.

On her journey, Hagar encounters an angel of the Lord (Genesis 16:7). The angel asks her where she is going, and she responds that she is fleeing from her mistress. The angel tells her to "return to your mistress and submit to her," (Genesis 16:9), and then makes her a promise:

"I will surely multiply your offspring so that they cannot be numbered for multitude."

And the angel of the Lord said to her,
"Behold, you are pregnant and shall bear a son. You shall
call his name Ishmael, because the Lord has listened to your
affliction. He shall be a wild donkey of a man, his hand against
everyone and everyone's hand against him, and he shall dwell over
against all his kinsmen."

Genesis 16:10-12

The Bible doesn't tell us about Hagar's inner life, her thoughts or feelings as she processes the challenges she has had to face. But we can guess from her words what happened within her when Hagar was confronted by the angel, because Hagar says to the angel of the Lord, "You are a God of seeing... truly here I have seen him who looks after me" (Genesis 16:13).

Hagar — a woman who was seen as foreign, strange, and less-than in her society, who was mistreated, abused, and too often overlooked — feels seen. She feels looked after. And when she returns to Sarah and gives birth to her son, she does as the angel told her and names him Ishmael. Because God listened.

Part Two: Hagar, Free

Chapters later, after Sarah and Abraham permanently banish Hagar and her son from their home, God yet again sees Hagar. As she weeps and lifts her voice, fearing the death of her son, the angel of God calls to her once again:

"What troubles you, Hagar? Fear not, for God has heard
the voice of the boy where he is. Up! Lift up the boy, and hold him
fast with your hand, for I will make him into a great nation."

Genesis 21:17

27

Hagar does so, and she and Ishmael survive in the wilderness. The last we hear of Hagar, she is finding an Egyptian wife for her son, providing for his future (Genesis 21:21). God kept His promises: a great people did rise from Ishmael.

In the eyes of her peers, Hagar was seen as a slave, a concubine, and among the lowest of people. But God saw Hagar, and he heard her cry. He made a way for her and her son in the desert. He fulfilled His promise.

Questions for contemplation:
1. When the angel of God spoke to Hagar in the wilderness, she called God "a God of seeing." How does God see and hear you, even when you may feel 'lost in the wilderness'?
2. Hagar was seen as less-than in her society. How does God see and hear those whom society rejects?
3. What might Hagar's story have to offer readers today?

Journaling prompt:
In the margins or on the pages of your Bible, reflect on today's readings. You may want to think about how God sees and hears His children, even and especially in times of need. For this, you could depict Hagar meeting the angel of the Lord, or hearing God's voice in the wilderness. You could also draw the "eyes" and "ears" of God, however you see them. You could also focus on Hagar's words, "you are a God of seeing," lettering or illustrating them. However you choose to journal this verse today is up to you: the Word is your canvas!

6

SARAH

This week's reading: Genesis 12, Genesis 17:15, Genesis 18:1-15, Genesis 21:1-7

This week's journaling focus: Genesis 18:9-14

Sarah is one of the few characters in the Bible whose name is changed by God. When we first meet her on the pages of Genesis 12, her name is Sarai, which means "my princess." She is married to a man named Abram, meaning "exalted father." How ironic, since he and Sarah have no children!

We know from reading Hagar's story last week that Sarai desperately wanted a child; but after many years of barrenness, she and Abram had likely given up on that wish. Little did they know that God would use them in the telling of His story, and that despite their age (and their doubts), their descendants would number as the stars in the sky and the sand on the shore. Abram would become Abraham, "father of many," and Sarai would become Sarah, a "princess" in her own right. Her wish— and God's promise — would be fulfilled. She would become the mother of nations.

Sarah's Story

Part One: Sarah and Abraham Travel to Egypt

Sarah's first mention in the Bible is in the context of a journey. In Genesis 12, God makes a covenant with Abraham, promising to make of him a great nation, and commanding him to leave his home, his people, and all that he knows, in favor of "the land that I will show you" (Genesis 12:1). It must have taken a great deal of faith on Abraham's part to say yes! Even greater faith was required, however, of Sarah; because while God spoke directly to Abraham, Sarah didn't receive such a revelation. She had to take the word of her seventy five-year-old husband that uprooting their lives and starting anew in an unnamed place, was a good idea.

But Abraham went, and Sarah followed. And so, the first thing that we learn about Sarah beside her name is that she trusts her husband. We learn in later verses that Sarah is a head-strong character; but in this verse, we see that her relationship with Abraham is one of give-and-take. In later chapters, Abraham may bow to Sarah's wishes, but in this verse, it is she who follows him.

Abraham and Sarah resettle in Canaan, where God makes another covenant (Genesis 12:7-8), and Abraham builds an altar to the Lord. However, a severe famine soon strikes the land, and Abraham and Sarah decide to move south to Egypt. Sarah is very beautiful, and Abraham is afraid to lose his life at the hands of the Egyptians. So, he concocts a plan:

> *"I know that you are a woman beautiful in appearance, and when the Egyptians see you, they will say, 'This is his wife.' Then they will kill me, but they will let you live. Say you are my sister, that it may go well with me because of you, and that my life may be spared for your sake."*
>
> Genesis 12:11-13

Abraham's lie is actually a half-truth: he and Sarah and half-siblings through their father, Terah. But in making Sarah lie and say that she is Abraham's sister, rather than his wife, Abraham is putting her in a dangerous position, risking her security and that of his future descendants. Sarah is taken into Pharaoh's house, and as a reward, Abraham is given servants, sheep, and camels (Genesis 12:16). As we find out in Genesis 12:19, Pharaoh takes Sarah "for my wife." But God interferes and sends plagues to Pharaoh's house, and to be free of the plagues, Pharaoh releases Sarah and Abraham so they can return to Canaan.

Part Two: Sarah and Hagar

We next hear of Sarah in the story of her and Hagar in Genesis 16. By the time this story takes place, God has already promised Abraham descendants multiple times over. But Sarah, perhaps doubting God's promise, or thinking that "God helps those who help themselves," takes matters into her own hands by sending Hagar to Abraham so that they can produce her an heir.

To understand why Sarah did this, it is important to understand why children were so important in Sarah's society. In a world in which women had very little autonomy or personal power, children were a way for a woman to procure a future for herself and her spouse. The child could care for the couple in their old age, and the couple's legacy would live on through that child and his descendants. Children were seen as a blessing, and sons especially were thought to be an honor to their mother.

Imagine, for a moment, the pressure Sarah is under as Abraham's wife. Abraham had been promised again and again by God that he would become the father of a great nation. As Abraham's wife, Sarah may feel that it is up to her to provide that nation for him; but she is barren. Her heartbreak over not having children is likely multiplied by the misplaced feeling that she is somehow disappointing her husband, or getting in the way of God's promise.

So Sarah tries to push the problem along, by pushing Hagar into Abraham's arms. Hagar does conceive a child, and thanks to her contemptuous looks Sarah's way, Sarah is thrown into a fit of rage, treating Hagar so harshly that she runs away. When Hagar comes back, she bears a son, Ishmael. Abraham and Sarah probably think that Ishmael will be the one through whom God fulfills His promise to them. But their story isn't over yet.

In Genesis 17, God changes the names of Abram and Sarai to Abraham and Sarah. He is preparing them for something. What that is, we find out just a few verses later.

Part Three: Sarah Laughed

Sarah's story reaches its climax in Genesis 18, when Abraham encounters three visitors: God in disguise. A gracious host, Abraham insists on bringing them water and bread, washing their feet, and letting them rest in the shade (Genesis 18:4). The guests ask Abraham where his wife, Sarah is. Abraham says she is in the tent, where Sarah is preparing cakes for their guests. Then God, disguised as the visitors, says,

> *"I will surely return to you about this time next year, and Sarah your wife shall have a son."*
>
> Genesis 18:10

Sarah overhears this from her tent. The Biblical text tells us that Abraham and Sarah were old, and that "the way of women had ceased to be with Sarah," meaning that she could no longer menstruate or have children (Genesis 18:11). So Sarah laughs to herself, asking, "After I am worn out and my lord is old, will I now have this pleasure?" (Genesis 18:12, NIV).

Put yourself in Sarah's shoes for a moment. The wish for a child was most likely a 'dream deferred' for Sarah. After decades of childlessness, she had probably given up hope that her wish would ever see the light of day.

Sarah may have laughed because she didn't believe God when He said she would bear a son. But laughter and emotion are a complicated thing, and mixed into her disbelief was probably a glimmer of hope. Could it be? Was it possible that after all these years, Sarah would have a child of her own, after all? If she let her imagination get far enough, in that split-second Sarah probably felt an intense joy at the prospect of new life within her, of little feet running through her tent. And maybe there was a touch of sadness. That this didn't happen when she was younger and better-able to enjoy new motherhood. That this didn't happen on her time.

Sarah's laugh was not just a giggle of disbelief. It was a likely a laugh of questioning, of hope, of joy, of confusion, of sadness. It is this moment where we can best imagine Sarah for who she is: a deeply human woman, experiencing God's hand over her life time and time again, and trying to keep up.

God overhears Sarah's laughter and asks, "'Why did Sarah laugh, and say, 'Shall I indeed bear a child, now that I am old?' Is anything too wonderful for the Lord?" (Genesis 18:13-14). He repeats the promise, and Sarah, most likely realizing only now that this is, in fact, God speaking to her, hastily takes back her laughter, saying that she didn't laugh. But God knows Sarah, and He heard her laugh and knew all that it meant and held. "Oh yes, you did laugh," He says.

From here, the Biblical text takes a detour and we learn about Sodom and Gomorrah, and in Genesis 20, Abraham's half-truth to Pharaoh somehow repeats itself. But sure enough, just a year after God's visit to Abraham and Sarah's tent, Sarah bears a son. She names him Isaac, which means laughter. And Sarah says, "God has brought laughter for me; everyone who hears will laugh with me" (Genesis 21:6 NRSV).

Sarah finally gets her deepest wish. She finally has her son — Isaac, her joy, her laughter.

Making Connections:

We have now studied Genesis 16 from both Hagar and Sarah's perspectives. We can see in these stories that Hagar and Sarah both looked at each other with jealousy and contempt. Hagar was likely jealous of Sarah's freedom, and may have resented Sarah for forcing her to conceive a child with Abraham. Sarah likely felt a deep jealousy towards Hagar for being able to bear the child that Sarah could not, and resented Hagar for the contemptuous looks she threw her way.

We can feel compassion to both Hagar and Sarah. Hagar, because she was a woman without power, who was abused, mistreated, and overlooked. Sarah, because her deepest wish went unfulfilled for decades, and because she had to see another woman have what she so desperately wanted.

How often have you experienced a similar anger towards another person? Have you ever felt superior, as Hagar felt towards Sarah? Have you ever resented, as Sarah resented Hagar for her gift of bearing children? How might Sarah and Hagar's story have ended differently if they had bonded over their shared differences? How did God see and hear both Sarah and Hagar, despite their human flaws?

Questions for Contemplation:

1. What do you think Sarah's laughter meant? Was it a laugh of disbelief? Joy? Hope? Sadness? All of the above?
2. Do you identify at all with Sarah and her story? Are there any dreams that you've given up on, or that have come true in God's timing and not your own?

Journaling Prompt:

Out of the long arc of Sarah's story, we will be journaling Genesis 18:9-14. In these verses, Sarah laughs, and God asks, "Is anything too wonderful for the Lord?"

You may wish to draw Sarah laughing, or illustrate through bright colors and textures the mix of emotions she must have felt when hearing God's promise. Or you could letter God's words, asking whether anything is too wonderful for God to accomplish or fulfill. Whichever direction you take, let the lessons and messages from Sarah's story find their way onto the page as you journal today.

7

REBECCA

This week's reading: Genesis 24, 25:19-34, 26:1-5, 27

This week's journaling focus: Genesis 24:15-21 OR Genesis
24:63-67

Rebecca never meets her mother-in-law, Sarah, but
in many ways she lives up to her legacy. Sarah and Rebecca
both love Isaac, though in very different ways: Sarah as a
mother, Rebecca as a wife. Through Abraham's blessing as
the father of God's people, Sarah and Rebecca each play a
major role in God's story, becoming mothers of that people
through God's promise. And both Sarah and Rebecca

are strong-willed women, who each take the fulfillment of God's promise into their own hands — for better or for worse.

But Rebecca is also very much her own person. She is unbelievably brave and bold, committing herself to a husband she has never met in a land she had never visited when she herself is still a girl (Genesis 24:58). She is beautiful both in appearance (Genesis 24:16) and, it seems, in spirit: Isaac loves Rebecca, and Rebecca is able to comfort him after his mother's death (Genesis 24:67). And, though she plays a manipulative part in the fulfillment of God's promise by tricking Isaac into blessing his younger son, unlike Sarah, Rebecca's meddling actually plays a role in fulfilling God's promise. She is imperfect, and there are parts of her story that may make us uncomfortable. But there is no doubt that God uses Rebecca in the telling of His story, and for that reason, she is important to us.

Rebecca's Story

Part One: Rebecca as Wife

A few major things happen between the telling of our last story, that of Sarah, and the story of Rebecca that we read today. The first is the Trial of Abraham, also called Binding of Isaac, a story that you may know well - if not, there are many wonderful resources to help you understand it! The second is Sarah's death in Genesis 23:1-2. This leaves us, at the beginning of Genesis 23, with an adult Isaac and an elderly Abraham. Abraham decides that it is time for his son to find a wife, so he goes to his oldest and most trusted servant and asks the servant to go to "my country and to my kindred" to find a wife suitable for his son. The servant travels to Abraham's homeland and stops outside the city, at a well. He says a prayer:

"O Lord, God of my master Abraham, please grant me success today and show steadfast love to my master Abraham. Behold, I am standing by the spring of water, and the daughters of the men of the city are coming out to draw water. Let the young woman to whom I shall say, 'Please let down your jar that I may drink,' and who shall say, 'Drink, and I will water your camels'—let her be the one whom you have appointed for your servant Isaac. By this I shall know that you have shown steadfast love to my master."

Genesis 24:12-14

Before the servant is even finished speaking, Rebecca appears with her water jug on her shoulder. She is described as a "young woman" and "very attractive in appearance;" some guess that she would have been in her mid-teens, significantly younger than the 40-year-old Isaac. The servant asks her for water, and she says "Drink, my Lord," and quickly takes her jug off her shoulder to offer him a drink (Genesis 24:18). When he is finished drinking, she draws water for all his ten camels; again, quickly. The servant stares at her in silence — or, perhaps, amazement — and knows that she is the one God intends to marry Isaac. We, in turn, know something, too: the character of Rebecca, who as a teenager is quick to help others, generous in her labor, and, as we soon find out, unafraid to make bold choices.

Several verses later, the servant is discussing the purpose of his journey with Rebecca's brother, Laban. They decide to ask Rebecca whether she would like to go with the servant to meet and marry the son of Abraham, who is a distant relative of hers. "Will you go with this man?" asks Laban in Genesis 24:58. "I will go," says Rebecca without missing a beat, and she does. Rebecca is not just helpful and generous, but also decisive and brave.

The love story between Rebecca and Isaac is one for the ages. Isaac and Rebecca see each other at a great distance, reminiscent of star-crossed lovers who see each other across a smokey room (Genesis 24:63-64). Isaac is told of her deeds, and he takes Rebecca into his mother's tent and takes her as his wife. We are told that "he loved her" and "was comforted after his mother's death" (Genesis 24:67).

While some might be confused at Isaac taking Rebecca into his mother's tent, I think it is a beautiful gesture. Isaac is welcoming her into the family. Rebecca is able to comfort him after his mother's death. It has been almost two full chapters since Sarah's passing, so we can assume that Isaac has been carrying this pain with him for quite some time. But Rebecca is able to comfort him, soothe his pain, and create a supportive foundation for their marriage. So we now know Rebecca to also be caring and comforting. What an amazing young woman she must have been.

Part Two: Rebecca as Mother

Rebecca is barren, but Isaac prays for her to become pregnant, and she does, in fact, conceive (Genesis 25:21). The pregnancy is not an easy one, however; Rebecca is pregnant with twins, and they wrestle within her, causing her to inquire with the Lord why this is happening (Genesis 25:22). God responds:

"Two nations are in your womb, and two peoples from within you shall be divided; the one shall be stronger than the other, the older shall serve the younger."

Genesis 25:23

For Rebecca to receive a revelation directly from God is truly amazing. She was not raised to know God; we know that her brother Laban worships idols (Genesis 31:19) and we can assume that Rebecca was taught to do the same. However, after marrying into Abraham's family, she has come to believe in God, and not only that, but rely on Him to answer her questions. She inquires with God, rather than simply complaining or being angry. Rebecca is truly a woman of faith.

This verse is important not only for that reason, however, but also because God appears to Rebecca and not Isaac. God trusts Rebecca with this knowledge, perhaps relying on the fact that certain character traits of hers would play a key role in the telling of God's story. In the ushering forth of His people, God uses and relies on this woman just as much, if not more so, than He relies on Isaac.

Rebecca does indeed have twins, and the younger, Jacob, is born clasping the foot of the older, Esau; almost as if he is vying for first place (Genesis 25:24-26). Just a few verses later, we learn just how true this is, as Jacob convinces a hungry Esau to give up his birthright for a bowl of soup (Genesis 25:39-34). To some, this reads as tricky and slimy on the part of Jacob, but it can also be read as a decisive comment on Esau, who was foolish enough to give up his birthright for dinner. Rebecca may have seen these qualities in her sons — Jacob slick, Esau foolish — before this story even occurred, because the Bible tells us that "Rebecca loved Jacob" (Genesis 25:28). Or maybe she loved Jacob for another reason, perhaps because she knew God had chosen the older, Esau, to serve the younger, Jacob.

Whatever the reason for her favoritism, its effects were certainly significant, as in Genesis 27 we see Rebecca trick her now-blind husband into bestowing his blessing upon Jacob, rather than his favored son, Esau. This is a moment in Rebecca's story that makes many of us, myself included, uncomfortable. How could Rebecca trade the success of one son for that of another?

However, it is possible that that was not Rebecca's intent; that instead, she made a tough choice to help along the future of God's people. Perhaps she knew her sons well, and knew that Esau may not have had the wisdom or character to carry out what was needed for the family that God chose. Or perhaps she was relying on the one time she heard the voice of God, when she was told that "the older will serve the younger" (Genesis 25:23). Whatever her reasoning, her choice is what lead to Jacob leaving home to find a wife, which lead him to marrying Leah and Rachel, which lead him to fathering the ancestors of the seven tribes of Israel.

Rebecca's actions, though certainly dubious and maybe even an indication of her lack of trust in God's hand at work, played an important role on the telling of God's story. Whatever her flaws, we can still respect her for that.

Making Connections:

Rebecca and Sarah share many traits, but one of the most interesting is the spirited initiative that they each take in the unfurling of their stories. Sarah tries to procure an heir through Hagar; Rebecca takes deceptive action to further the interests of one child and not the other. As we have seen in the last two weeks, Sarah's actions were not integral to she herself having a son; as we see in Genesis 18 and 21, it is Sarah's God, not her actions, that give her a son.

However, Rebecca's choice is more directly significant to the future of God's people, because it is through her actions that Jacob meets his wives and eventually becomes father to the sons who become the ancestors of Israel's seven tribes.

How do Sarah's and Rebecca's motives differ when they make these choices? Are they the same? How does God use Rebecca's personal characteristics to further His purposes? How could God make use of our own strengths, weaknesses, and imperfections?

Questions for Contemplation:
1. Did Rebecca's manipulation lack trust in God's plan, or show her commitment to its fulfillment?
2. Which of Rebecca's character traits are ones that you respect or admire? Are there any that you think less of?
3. Rebecca is a strong and decisive woman, acting in her own story. These qualities can be both good and bad. How does God make use of them in both their good and bad applications to tell His story?

Journaling Prompt:
Rebecca's patience, kindness, and generosity at the well are what lead her to be chosen as Isaac's wife, which in turn made her an important link in the long chain of God's people, leading from Abraham to Jacob all the way down to David and, eventually, Jesus. For this pivotal moment of

Rebecca's life, you may choose to illustrate her offering a drink to the stranger, or water to his camels. Alternatively, you could choose to draw her and Isaac seeing each other for the first time. Choose the moment which speaks more to you, and reflect on the words and images as you journal.

8

LEAH

This week's reading: Genesis 29:16-35; 30:9-21; 31:4, 14, 17; 33:2-7; Ruth 4:11

This week's journaling focus: Genesis 29:35

In last week's study, we learned about Rebecca and her two sons, Jacob and Esau. Jacob and Esau are twins, and they are born with Jacob clutching the heel of his older brother, as though he is vying to be first. This later turns out to be true; as young men, Jacob tricks his brother into giving away his birthright in exchange for a bowl of soup

(Genesis 25:29-34). But the old saying applies: what goes around comes around. Only a few years later, Jacob, too, is deceived — and, with a touch of irony, this deception involves a pair of sisters, who may themselves also have been twins, according to some traditions.

But the story of Leah and Rachel is about far more than Jacob's deception. It is a narrative of joy and grief, of life and death, and of the love and competition that can arise between sisters. However, as much as they were filled with jealousy and competition, we may be reminded of the words of the elders in the Book of Ruth: "Rachel and Leah... together built up the house of Israel" (Ruth 4:11). They lived their lives in competition, and didn't always work with each other, but Rachel and Leah built a lasting legacy — together.

Leah's Story

Leah and Rachel's stories are so intertwined that it is difficult to study one and not the other, so as we journal alongside Leah today, you will also get a taste of Rachel's side of the story.

Part One: A Loveless Marriage

Rachel and Leah were the daughters of Laban, who we encountered last week as Rebecca's brother. They lived with servants and livestock in Canaan. Rachel, the younger sister, was "beautiful in form and appearance" (Genesis 29:17), but all we know of Leah's appearance is her eyes. The word used to describe them has been translated many different ways. Sometimes "fair" or "lovely," other times "soft" or "weak." Perhaps her eyes were Leah's defining feature, bringing beauty to an otherwise plain countenance. Even if they had been weak, they would have stood out, because as we will soon learn, Leah was a strong woman, made of grit and resilience.

Leah and Rachel probably lived fairly routine lives in their father's home, with the same habits and events repeating themselves day in and day out. We can only imagine the excitement and confusion on the day that Jacob entered their lives, weary and worn from his journey through the desert. All the more confusing was his entrance: upon seeing Rachel at the well, he kissed her and wept.

Jacob was brought back to Laban and struck a deal with him: in exchange for seven years' labor, he could marry Rachel. The Bible tells us that those seven years "seemed to him but a few days because of the love he had for her" (Genesis 29:20). A beautiful description of a love that ran deep.

At the end of Jacob's seven years of labor, the story takes a dramatic turn. When Jacob comes to Laban to ask for his new wife, Laban throws a great feast, but doesn't bring him Rachel. Instead, Jacob wakes up the next morning, and "behold, it was Leah!" beside him (Genesis 29:25). Many have wondered what could have happened that night. J. Ellsworth Kalas suggests that Jacob so drunk that he couldn't tell the difference between his beloved and her sister. The midrashic tradition of Jewish biblical interpretation wonders if maybe Rachel was whispering outside the tent, so Jacob heard her voice in the dark. Author Anita Diamante puts forth in The Red Tent that maybe Jacob knew about the switch, but allowed it to be so. We don't know exactly what happened that night, but we do know what happens the next morning: he goes to Laban and demands that justice be done. The following week, he marries Rachel, in exchange for seven more years of service.

This is how Leah and her sister Rachel end up married to the same man. The Bible doesn't mince words about Jacob's affections: "he loved Rachel more than Leah" (Genesis 29:30).

We know that Leah loved Jacob, and craved his affections. We can only imagine how it must have felt for her to have watched him toiling in labor to win Rachel's hand, while she herself was overlooked. Being given to him in marriage, but only due to a deceitful trick on her father's part. Being given the man she loved, and the very next week seeing him marry her sister, Rachel.

So Leah's story begins in sadness. But soon, we will see her brought to life with love: not from her husband, but from her children.

Part Two: A Loving Family

While Rachel remains barren, Leah has child after child. First is Reuben, "Because the Lord has looked upon my affliction; for now my husband will love me" (Genesis 29:32).

And still, Jacob doesn't love her.

Next is Simeon, "Because the Lord has heard that I am hated, he has given me this son also." (Genesis 29:33).

And still, Leah is unloved.

Third is Levi, "Now this time my husband will be attached to me, because I have borne him three sons" (Genesis 29:34).

And still, Jacob remains unattached.

Finally is Judah. With his birth, Leah says "This time I will praise the Lord" (Genesis 29:35). Leah was not born in to Jacob's faith; rather, she adopted it as her own when she married him. Here we see, however, that Leah truly was a woman of faith, who praises the Lord with every birth of her children, and mentions God in these chapters more often than any other figure. She took the faith of her husband and made it her own. Rebecca would have been proud.

Jacob may not have loved Leah, but God saw and heard Leah, and he blessed her through family. Leah's handmaiden, Zilpah, has two sons for Jacob, and Leah eventually bears another three children: two sons, Issachar and Zebulun, and finally a daughter, Dinah. And just as Leah for years had to watch her sister Rachel be loved and adored by Jacob, now Rachel watches in jealousy as Leah has a family of her own and Rachel remains barren. Rachel eventually does have two sons; but we'll save that story for next week.

Leah may not have received the love of her husband, and her life was not without trials. But we know that she was brought honor and love through her children, and they brought her joy. When Leah's handmaiden Zilpah has two sons of Jacob, Leah sings of her "good fortune" and even says, "happy am I! For women have called me happy" (Genesis 30:13).

Children are also how Leah creates a lasting legacy. Her sons become the fathers of most of the tribes of Israel. It is through these children that the blessing of Abraham is passed down: first to Isaac, then Jacob, and then to Jacob's twelve sons, through, among others, Leah.

Their lives may have felt small and inconsequential on the day that Jacob first entered their world at the well. But ultimately, the words of the Book of Ruth ring true: "Rachel and Leah... together built up the house of Israel" (Ruth 4:11).

49

Making Connections

Here's a little reminder from last week's study on Rebecca:

"[Rebecca] was not raised to know God; we know that her brother Laban worships idols (Genesis 31:19) and we can assume that Rebecca was taught to do the same. However, after marrying into Abraham's family, she has come to believe in God, and not only that, but rely on Him to answer her questions. She inquires with God, rather than simply complaining or being angry. Rebecca is truly a woman of faith."

While we don't get the chance to hear Leah pray, through the names of her children, we can see that she has a strong faith in God, as well. Though her first three sons are named in the hope that she will receive the love of her husband, when she names Judah, she says, "This time I will praise the Lord" (Genesis 29:35).

Rebecca and Leah both came from a home outside Jacob's faith, where idols were worshipped. Both show through their prayers and praises that they find support and joy in God even when trying circumstances trouble them. How might we learn from their example to find joy even in hard times?

Questions for Contemplation

1. Leah had to watch her sister, Rachel, receive love while she did not. Rachel had to watch Leah have children while she remained barren. Have you ever been in a position where you had to watch another person receive love or blessings that you yourself wanted? How did you deal with that?

2. When Jacob dies at the end of Genesis, he is buried next to Leah, rather than next to Rachel. Though Jacob loved Rachel more in life, he chose to honor Leah more in death. How might this final note on Leah's story change how you see her?

3. Though Leah had many children and gifts, she is often best remembered for not receiving the love of her husband. God saw what Leah "lacked" and still built her up and honored her through family and a lasting legacy. How might God see and honor us despite what we feel we "lack"?

Journaling Prompt:

When three children still didn't bring her the love of her husband, Leah named her son Judah, to "praise the Lord" full stop, with no conditions. We will be journaling Genesis 29:35 this week, when Leah says, "This time, I will praise the Lord." You may choose to illustrate Leah in praise, holding her newborn son. Or you may choose to letter her words at Judah's birth. Finally, if there was another part of this story that resonated with you, you may choose to illustrate or dwell on that. Don't let your inhibitions hold you back as your journal today. Whatever you may feel you "lack" in skill, God still sees and hears you just as you are.

9

RACHEL

This week's reading: Genesis 29:9-31; 30:1, 22-26; 31:1-3, 17-21, 33-35; 35:18-20, Ruth 4:11

This week's journaling focus: Ruth 4:11

Rachel was Jacob's second wife, but was anything but secondary in his eyes. Jacob loved Rachel and would have done anything to make her happy. Still, her story is not without sadness: more than anything, Rachel wanted a child, but for years she had to watch her sister Leah have children while she stayed barren.

Because the stories of Rachel and Leah are so intertwined, in the last chapter we were able to see parts of Rachel's story through Leah's perspective. This chapter is a continuation of the previous readings in more ways than one. We will read about Rachel's life, but also about her legacy and that of Leah: how they intertwined, and the roles they played in the future of God's people.

A Closing Note on the Matriarchs

Rachel is the last woman of Genesis who we will study as part of our Women of Valor series. These women, who include Hagar as well as the four Matriarchs — Sarah, Rebecca, Leah, and Rachel — were each known and remembered in large part because of their children. For many of us, that may be a difficult pill to swallow, because not all of our stories end as Sarah's did, with our prayers for children or other lifelong dreams answered in the ways that we want. But is important to remember that these women are remembered as mothers in large part because of the time in which Genesis was written. Just as each of us leaves a beautiful and rich legacy made of relationships, home, creativity, and wisdom, the Matriarchs' legacies were broader than the children they had. These legacies also include the lessons they teach us now. Today, we read Rachel's story with that idea of a richer 'legacy' in mind.

Rachel's Story

Part One: Rachel's Life

Rachel was Leah's sister: "beautiful in form and

appearance" (Genesis 29:17), and loved deeply by Jacob. When she encountered Jacob at the well, she was only a young girl. After he kissed her and wept, he went to her father and exchanged seven years of labor for her hand in marriage. As we learned last week, on the night of his intended wedding to Rachel, he instead was given Leah, something that Jacob only realized or addressed in the morning light (Genesis 29:25). So he went to their father, Laban, to see that justice be done. One week later, he married Rachel, in exchange for seven more years of service.

In marriage, Rachel was given the love that Leah wanted; but for years, she went without the children she so desperately wanted. This divide turned Rachel and Leah into not just sisters, not just women who shared the same man, but also into rivals, battling each other for their husband's affection and children. Finally, after what seems to have been many years of waiting, Rachel conceives a son. In her joy at finding out, she cries, "God has taken away my reproach," (Gen 30:23) and when her son is born, she names him Joseph, in the hopes that "the Lord [may] add to me another son" (Gen 30:24).

After Rachel has her son, Jacob goes to Laban and asks that he and his wives be allowed to return to Jacob's home country in exchange for his many years of service. But Laban feels that he has been blessed by Jacob's labor, so instead he makes a counter-offer, saying that he will give Jacob anything he asks for in wages. Jacob stays and grows his own flock of sheep and livestock. But after he hears Laban's sons speaking of him with bitterness, he decides to leave, and hears the voice of the Lord saying that God will be with him (Genesis 31:1-3).

So Jacob sets his wives on camels and gathers his livestock to leave. But before they do, when Laban is shearing sheep, Rachel goes into his house and steals his idols. We don't know why this was; perhaps to spite him, or maybe because she herself still used idols instead of or in addition to worshipping Jacob's God. When Laban goes after them to retrieve his idols, Rachel sits on them and pretends that she is menstruating and cannot get up (Genesis 31:33-35). So Rachel protects her family from the ramifications of her stealing, through a lie. Perhaps not something we would expect from one of the most celebrated mothers of our faith!

During the journey, Rachel conceives again and finally has her much-wanted second son. However, the labor is too difficult for her, and this is where Rachel meets her end. With her dying breath, she names her son Ben-Oni, meaning "son of my sorrow," but Jacob renames him Benjamin, or "son of my right hand." And "so Rachel died, and she was buried on the way to Ephrath (that is, Bethlehem)" (Genesis 35:19) left in a middle-place between her family's past and future, much as she was in a middle-place between joy and sorrow for much of her life.

Part Two: Rachel's Legacy

Still, despite the sad end to Rachel's life, her story lives on through her sons. Her first son, Joseph, is favored by Jacob and thus sold into slavery by his brothers, but rises from slavery to become an overseer of Egypt. He also becomes a strong and confident leader much like his father, and reconciles with his brothers despite their betrayal. He and Rachel's other son Benjamin, along with Leah's sons and those of their handmaidens Zilpah and Bilhah, become the heads of the Twelve Tribes of Israel and so the fathers of God's people.

Rachel was an imperfect woman. She kept idols,

which tells us that her faith was likely less strong than Leah's, or that her long-lasting infertility perhaps caused her to trust less in God. She was bitter towards her sister, though the sour parts of their relationship were two-sided just as much as were the loving parts. And she was not naturally resilient, often complaining or lashing out at her loved ones such as when she yells at Jacob, "Give me children, or I shall die!"

And still, despite her imperfections, she was chosen to be one of the mothers of God's people. Along with Sarah, Rebecca, and Leah, Rachel is considered one of the matriarchs. She is still remembered today, honored in homes around the world on the night of the Jewish sabbath, when daughters are blessed with the words,

"May God make you like Sarah, Rebecca, Rachel and Leah."

Though Rachel may have felt forgotten when God did not give her children, she was always remembered, just as God remembered Hagar, and Sarah, and Rebecca, and Leah in their own distress. And still today, we remember her.

Making Connections

As matriarchs in the Judeo-Christian tradition, both Leah and Rachel had lasting legacies through their children; but they also offer us a legacy of lessons, teaching us how and how not to respond to life's trials. Though Leah is often thought of as the forgotten or overlooked sister, Rachel's life is also deeply challenging, in part because of her response to difficulty. How do Rachel and Leah respond to challenges differently? How do their differing responses to challenges shape their lives?

Questions for Contemplation

1. Rachel deals with a lot of sadness and jealousy because of her rivalry with Leah, which was likely made worse by the fact that the two women were sisters. How could their close relationship have eased their burdens, rather than worsening them if they had responded to this situation differently?

2. Rachel and Leah's legacies are most often seen as being through their children, but as we saw in 'Making Connections,' they also offer another kind of legacy. What is your legacy? Is it your work? Your family? Your creativity? Is it the kindness with which you live your life? How would you like to be remembered by those who know you?

Journaling Prompt:

Rachel's legacy through her sons is what the elders in the Book of Ruth refer to when they say that "Rachel and Leah... together built up the house of Israel" (Ruth 4:11), a verse that we also encountered last week. When I hear this, I imagine these two sisters building up a castle, taking turns laying the stones brick-by-brick. You may choose to illustrate this verse in that way, or you may decide that you would like to take the verse in a more personal direction by reflecting on your own legacy. What have you 'built' in your life, through work, family, or relationships? Consider journaling that today, illustrating your family or friends, or even a self-portrait of you Bible journaling as you leave behind a legacy of faith. Finally, you may choose to letter the word 'legacy' in the margin of your Bible, surrounded by meaningful words or phrases that relate to the legacy you hope to leave behind. Have fun!

10

MIRIAM

This week's reading: Exodus 2:1-10, 15:20-21 ; Numbers 12:1-15; Micah 6:4

This week's journaling focus: Exodus 15:20-21

Miriam: sister, protector, prophetess. Her name means 'bitter sea,' but the word bitter can also mean strong. In some ways, Miriam was a sea of strength, watching over her younger brother Moses as he was hidden in the reeds of the Nile when she herself was still a young girl (Exodus 2:1-10). But in others, her tenacity and stubbornness worked like waves crashing over the shore, eroding the patience of those around her (Numbers 12:1-15). The same qualities that brought her to lead the Israelite women in joyful dance (Exodus 15:20-21), led to her punishment in the desert. And yet, she is remembered, for both her stubbornness and leadership:

> *For I brought you up from the land of Egypt   and redeemed you from the house of slavery, and I sent before you Moses,   Aaron, and Miriam.*

Micah 6:4

Join us this week in the story of Miriam, who God sent before us.

Miriam's Story

Part One: A Young Girl

Generations after Rachel, her descendants through Joseph are living in slavery and oppression in Egypt. The pharaoh he fears that the Hebrew people have grown too strong and numerous, so he issues a decree that "Every son that is born to the Hebrews you shall cast into the Nile, but you shall let every daughter live" (Exodus 1:22).

This is the world that the baby Moses is born into. His mother, whose name is Jocheved, hides Moses for the first three months of his life, but knows that she would not be able to hide him any longer. So she places him in a basket in the reeds long the Nile and leaves him there, with no one to look after him — no one, except Miriam. Miriam is only a young girl, but she takes on a responsibility that

59

will end up shaping the history of God's people.

The pharaoh's daughter is walking along the Nile when she sees the basket. Upon opening it, she knows immediately that this is one of the Hebrew children, and takes pity on him. Miriam must have noted the softness in her voice, because she approaches the daughter of the pharaoh and asks, "Shall I go and call you a nurse from the Hebrew women to nurse the child for you?" (Exodus 2:7). When the pharaoh's daughter agrees, Miriam fetches her mother, and in this way, Moses is able to be nursed by his mother just a bit longer, before he is raised by the pharaoh's daughter.

Though we haven't yet heard Miriam's name, we can learn of her character from this episode. She is protective, brave, and bold — bold enough to approach the daughter of the most powerful man in her empire, and skilled enough with her words to do so in a way that ends favorably for her family.

Part Two: A Young Woman

We find out more of her story decades later, when Moses has delivered the Hebrew people from slavery in Egypt. Finally we learn Miriam's name: "Miriam the prophetess, the sister of Aaron," who is the brother of Moses (Exodus 15:20). We know that is a prophetess, not only from her title, but also from her behavior; shortly after the Hebrew people are delivered from Egypt, she leads the Hebrew women in song and dance:

Then Miriam the prophetess, the sister of Aaron, took a tambourine in her hand, and all the women went out after her with tambourines and dancing. And Miriam sang to them: "Sing to the Lord, for he has triumphed gloriously; the horse and his rider he has thrown into the sea."

Exodus 15:20-21

Decades after her first act of bravery on the banks of the River Nile, Miriam still displays the skills of leadership and bravery as she boldly leads the Hebrew women in dance. This after generations of slavery, and what was surely a challenging and often bitter life for Miriam, who was herself also a slave. Even after being released from such trauma, not many of us would have the spirit to sing God's praises, as Miriam does here. Fewer still would have the heart to lead such a group in worship.

And still, Miriam does. A life of slavery has not extinguished her bold and celebratory spirit. She uses her gift of leadership to sing the praises of the Lord, to celebrate His triumph.

Part Three: A Moment Regretted, a Lifetime Remembered

But Miriam's boldness and leadership bring her both glory and trouble. Chapters later, in the book of Numbers, she and Aaron speak against Moses to complain about his Cushite wife; at least, on the surface. Angrily, they also say "Has the Lord indeed spoken only through Moses? Has he not spoken through us also?", implying that perhaps jealousy was also the cause of the bitter conversation (Numbers 12:2). God hears them and reprimands them for their words. When He disappears, Moses and Aaron are the same, but Miriam has been struck with leprosy. Aaron pleads with Moses, who tries to intercede with God on Miriam's behalf, but He does not change His mind. Miriam must wait outside the camp for seven days, and the Israelites do not move until she can rejoin them.

Many have wondered why Miriam is the only one punished for what she and Aaron did. Interestingly, the Bible tells us that "Miriam and Aaron spoke against Moses;" not Aaron first and Miriam second, as would have been a more common phrasing in that time (Numbers 12:1). The fact that Miriam is named first implies that here, too, she was a leader; that perhaps it was she who spoke first, or who egged Aaron on. Maybe her leadership in this act of judgment and bitterness explains the unequal punishment between her and her brother.

This is the last we hear of Miriam's story before her death in Numbers 20:1. But there is a final line in the Hebrew Bible that remembers her, in the book of Micah:

> *For I brought you up from the land of Egypt and redeemed you from the house of slavery, and I sent before you Moses, Aaron, and Miriam.*
>
> Micah 6:4

Moses, Aaron, and Miriam. She had her flaws, and her life was unduly difficult, but she is not forgotten. Though she is not one of the matriarchs of Genesis, her name is still carried on today as theirs are, given to girls in both the Christian and Jewish tradition. In them, her life and legacy live on.

Making Connections

Miriam is the sixth woman we have studied as part of our Women of Valor series. Each woman before her — Hagar, Sarah, Rebecca, Leah, and Rachel — was chosen by God for a special purpose in the story of His people, despite her flaws. In some cases, God overlooked traits like doubt to make use of ordinary women like Sarah. In others, He took qualities that could be either good or bad, and used them to unfold His story, like with Rebecca. And in still others, God remembered the women whom the world forgot, like Hagar and Leah.

Miriam fits into this framework. Her brashness, while punished in Numbers, was ultimately forgiven: Miriam was still considered a prophetess, and she was still sent before us, remembered for her song and not her mistake. Her boldness and leadership, while sometimes troublesome, were also used to help her lead the Hebrew women in praise. And while the world forgot Miriam and the other Hebrew people enslaved in Egypt, God remembered them, and delivered them from their oppression.

Questions for Contemplation

1. It is easy to doubt God's promises as they apply to our own lives. How do the stories of imperfect women, who were still heroines in God's story, remind us that our own weaknesses can be overlooked or used for a greater purpose?

2. Miriam's weakness of brash speech tied in to her gift of leadership in worship and community. Could any of your weaknesses have an upside in how you serve God's people?

3. Miriam used her gift of leadership to lead the women of her community in a song of praise. Which of your qualities might have been given to you for the purpose of serving others?

4. Like Hagar was overlooked in Hebrew society, Miriam was seen as "less-than" by Egyptian society. How does Miriam's story tie in to Jesus'

command to love and remember "the least of these" (Matthew 25:40)? How might we use our gifts to help the Hagars and Miriams of our world today?

Journaling Prompt:

Though you are welcome to journal any portion of Miriam's story that stood out to you, this week our community will be focusing on Miriam's leading of the the song in Exodus 15:20-21. You may want to illustrate a crowd of women dancing in praise of God, either in an ancient Israelite setting, or women today from all around the world. You could also focus on how Miriam used her gifts to bring glory to God, journaling an entry that uses your gifts to bring glory to God in the same way. Finally, you could focus on the words of the verse: "Sing to the Lord, for he has triumphed gloriously," lettering them or showing the ways that God has triumphed in your life. Reflect on this story and use your thoughts to guide you as you journal today.

11

RUTH

This week's reading: The Book of Ruth; Matthew 1:5

This week's journaling focus: Ruth 2:12

Most Biblical characters come with a caveat. Sarah was loving, but she was doubtful; Rebecca was brave, but headstrong; Rachel lovely, but jealous; Miriam caring and careless. We each have our favorites, but recognize that their strengths come with weakness. Not so, seemingly, for Ruth. Of all the women in the Bible, she has stood out to generations for her bravery, loyalty, and humility. She is the only Biblical woman who is directly called an the eshet chayil: a woman of worth, a woman of valor (Ruth 3:11).

All this, despite the fact that she in many ways defied the typical expectations of women both in her day and today. She was a foreigner, a widow, and a convert. And yet, her character and actions proved that no outside label define your worth. Let's read more about this brave and extraordinary woman, and the role she plays in God's story.

Ruth's Story

Part One: A Time of Famine

Ruth's story takes place in "the days when the judges ruled," when "there was a famine in the land." You may be familiar with the Book of Judges as being one of the darkest in the Bible: the stories in those pages are enough to make you ache and weep. This is a time of moral and literal famine. Israel is suffering from a political disaster as hunger sweeps through the land.

To escape the famine in Israel, a man named Elimelech takes his wife Naomi and his two sons, Mahlon and Chilion, to the country of Moab. This is, in itself, not the silver lining. Moab is the sworn enemy of Israel, and had been for generations, ever since the Hebrew people had escaped from slavery in Egypt and the Moabites had cursed them. Some have speculated that it was Elimelech's lack of faith in God that sent him to Moab, or his inability to deal with hardship. Whatever the reason, their temporary situation becomes a permanent one when both sons marry Moabite women: Orpah and Ruth.

But the time of happiness that we hope surrounds these unions soon turns to sorrow. Elimelech, Mahlon, and Chilion die, leaving Naomi, a wife and mother, widowed and childless. Few can imagine such trauma, and as we see from her words, Naomi is devastated and grief-stricken. But that is about to change.

Naomi chooses to return to her homeland of Israel. Orpah and Ruth want to go with her, but Naomi tries to convince them otherwise:

"Turn back, my daughters; why will you go with me? Have I yet sons in my womb that they may become your husbands? Turn back, my daughters; go your way, for I am too old to have a husband. If I should say I have hope, even if I should have a husband this night and should bear sons, would you therefore wait till they were grown? Would you therefore refrain from marrying? No, my daughters, for it is exceedingly bitter to me for your sake that the hand of the Lord has gone out against me."

Ruth 1:11-14

Her words convince Orpah, who tearfully leaves Naomi to return alone to Israel. But not so for Ruth. Despite Naomi's urging, despite the challenging road that lies ahead of her, and despite her clearly devastated heart — or maybe because of those things — Ruth chooses to stay with Naomi. When doing so, she utters a poem that is still remembered and recited at weddings to this day:

"Do not urge me to leave you or to return from following you. For where you go I will go, and where you lodge I will lodge. Your people shall be my people, and your God my God. Where you die I will die, and there will I be buried. May the Lord do so to me and

more also if anything but death parts me from you."

Ruth 1:16-17

Naomi gives in, and together, they return to Israel. The text tells us that this happens as the barley harvest is beginning, and just as those crops indicate a return to fullness and plenty, they indicate a turning point in our story.

Part Two: A Time of Fullness

In Israel lives a man named Boaz, who is a distant relative of Naomi's. Naomi instructs Ruth to go to Boaz's field and glean from the edges of his crop. When Boaz enters his field to interact with his workers, he calls to them, "The Lord be with you!" (Ruth 2:4). He is, then, a man of faith.

Boaz notices Ruth immediately, and is struck when he hears that she has been hard at work all day. He gives her special instructions and provisions for working in his field, to keep her safe and give her enough grain. Humbled and confused, Ruth asks, "Why have I found favor in your eyes, that you should take notice of me, since I am a foreigner?" (Ruth 2:10). Boaz responds:

"All that you have done for your mother-in-law since the death of your husband has been fully told to me, and how you left your father and mother and your native land and came to a people that you did not know before. The Lord repay you for what you have done, and a full reward be given you by the Lord, the God of Israel, under whose wings you have come to take refuge!"

Ruth 2:11-12

Boaz doesn't see her as a foreigner, a widow, or a

68

convert, each of which could caused him to overlook her or cast her out. Instead, he sees her for her character and her actions. When Boaz looks at Ruth, he doesn't judge her by the color of her skin, her accent, or her newness to his country or belief. He recognizes her strength, courage, loyalty, and her faith in the Lord God, in whom she has found refuge. He commends her for what she has accomplished, rather than condemning her for her societal labels. In this way, Boaz demonstrates the encompassing love and mercy that God, too, shows us.

As a lover of romantic comedies and happy endings, I tingle with excitement at this encounter between Ruth and Boaz. Naomi's reaction must have been similar, but with an added lining of hope: Boaz is a distant relative of hers, and if Ruth plays her cards right, the two can get married and secure a future for both Ruth and Naomi. Through Naomi's instructions and Boaz's cunning, we see just this happen in Ruth 4, as Boaz "redeems" the widowed Ruth, and marries her. The two have a son, who according to the law of the time belonged to Naomi. You can almost hear the words 'and they lived happily ever after' echo in your ears, but there's just one bit more.

He was the father of Jesse, the father of David.
Ruth 4:17

Ruth's son becomes the father of Jesse, the father of David, who becomes the ancestor of Jesus. This is how a young Moabite woman — foreign, widowed, and only recently converted to the Israelite faith — becomes the ancestress of our own redeemer. Ruth's loyalty to Naomi led her to find comfort and refuge under the wings of God, and for that, she is honored her as a great woman of our faith.

Making Connections

Like Hagar, Ruth was a foreign woman who had every reason to be judged and excluded by her Israelite neighbors. There are differences between these two women, of course, but also parallels for what they teach us about the overlooked or hurt children of God.

When reading Hagar's story, our group focused on how God sees and hears us, even when we may feel lost in the desert. But God doesn't appear directly to Ruth during her trials. Instead, God shows Himself through the love, kindness, and generosity of Boaz. While Ruth may inspire us to live lives of loyalty and bravery, Boaz reminds us of the importance of acting with kindness and generosity towards the unseen and overlooked.

Questions for Contemplation

1. Naomi experiences tremendous heartbreak that later turned into a new beginning. Does this story give you any hope for a situation you may be dealing with in your own life?

2. Through their trials and travels, Ruth and Naomi most likely found immense comfort in their relationship with each other. Who is someone in your life who brings you comfort during hard times?

3. Boaz remarks that Ruth has found refuge under the wings of God. Many are drawn to this verse for its beautiful imagery, which reminds us that even in our times of famine, we can find comfort in the one who redeems us. What practices might help you find comfort in God in tough times?

Journaling Prompt:

There is so much to Ruth's story, as the length of this week's reading suggests. Of the many inspiring and beautiful verses we encountered today, our group will be focusing on Ruth 2:12: "The Lord repay you for what you have done, and a full reward be given you by the Lord, the God of Israel, under whose wings you have come to take refuge!" You may wish to illustrated a bird here, either in flight or nestling something under its protective wings. You could also choose to use imagery of feathers sweeping you up or cradling you. Finally, you may choose to letter the words of the verse. Do whatever feels appropriate to you for this verse today.

12

HANNAH

This week's reading: 1 Samuel 1, 1 Samuel 2:1-10

This week's journaling focus: 1 Samuel 2:2

Often, the women we have encountered throughout this study are called 'Women of Faith.' This description is sometimes true, and sometimes less apt; but in Hannah's case, she has truly earned the title. Like many women in our study, Hannah desperately wanted a child, but remained barren. Both in her barrenness and after her son's eventual birth, Hannah turned to God to pray. Today we study those prayers and what they mean for us today. Join us in journaling with Hannah, the woman who prayed.

Hannah's Story

Part One: A Prayer of Petition

In the hill lands of Ephraim lives a man named Elkanah and his two wives, Hannah and Peninnah. Peninnah has children, and Hannah does not; due to the culture around having children at that time, the difference could make one wife seem more valuable than the other to their husband. But Elkanah loves Hannah, giving her double portions on the day he sacrifices (1 Samuel 1:5). Her barrenness doesn't matter to him, but it mattered to Peninnah, who uses it to taunt Hannah mercilessly year after year (1 Samuel 1:6). The taunting hurts Hannah, causing her to weep and stop eating. Elkanah tries to comfort her, but she cannot not be comforted.

Elkanah and Hannah go to Shiloh to worship. One morning, Hannah rises and goes to the temple of the Lord to pray. The text tells us that "she was deeply distressed and prayed to the Lord and wept bitterly (1 Samuel 1:10). In prayer, she makes a vow, saying:

"O Lord of hosts, if you will indeed look on the affliction of your servant and remember me and not forget your servant, but will give to your servant a son, then I will give him to the Lord all the days of his life, and no razor shall touch his head."

1 Samuel 1:11

Hannah is serious in her vow: her promise not to let a razor touch her son's head reflects her decision to raise him as a Nazarite, or an Israelite who dedicates his life to the Lord by abstaining from drinking, cutting hair, and bodily defilement through the touching of the deceased (Numbers 6:1-21, with special attention to Numbers 6:5).

We also know that her prayer wasn't uttered in a passionless or dry way. Instead, she is wailing; "speaking in her heart," moving her mouth silently in such a way that the priest Eli thinks she is drunk (1 Samuel 1:12-13). When Eli berates her, she responds, "No, my lord, I am a woman troubled in spirit. I have drunk neither wine nor strong drink, but I have been pouring out my soul before the Lord. Do not regard your servant as a worthless woman, for all along I have been speaking out of my great anxiety and vexation." (1 Samuel 1:15-16). Eli says to her, "Go in peace, and the God of Israel grant your petition that you have made to him," and when Hannah leaves, she eats, no longer sad (1 Samuel 1:17-18).

The next morning, Hannah and her husband Elkanah wake up and worship the Lord before returning home to Ramah. When they return, Hannah conceives and has a son, naming him Samuel: "I have asked for him from the Lord" (1 Sam 1:20).

Part Two: A Prayer of Thanksgiving

Some time later, Elkanah and his house make their yearly trip to sacrifice and make vows to the Lord. Hannah, however, does not join him. Instead, she says, "As soon as the child is weaned, I will bring him, so that he may appear in the presence of the Lord and dwell there forever" (1 Samuel 1:22). When Samuel is weaned, she takes him to the priest Eli, and says:

74

"Oh, my lord! As you live, my lord, I am the woman who was standing here in your presence, praying to the Lord. For this child I prayed, and the Lord has granted me my petition that I made to him. Therefore I have lent him to the Lord. As long as he lives, he is lent to the Lord."

1 Sam 1:26-28

Her prayer is answered, and she keeps her vow. So, too, does Samuel, because as the text tells us, "he worshipped the Lord there" (1 Sam 1:28). But the story isn't over. Before she departs, Hannah issues a prayer of thanksgiving.

"My heart exults in the Lord;
my horn is exalted in the Lord.
My mouth derides my enemies,
because I rejoice in your salvation.
There is none holy like the Lord:
for there is none besides you;
there is no rock like our God."

1 Samuel 2:1-2

Those of us familiar with Mary's prayer of thanksgiving, known as the Magnificat, will hear echoes of that in Hannah's first line. But the poem is Hannah's own, and the imagery is rich and vivid. Just as her prayer of petition was fervent and passionate, this one comes from the heart. In good times and bad, Hannah turns to the Lord. That legacy lives on in her son Samuel, a godly man and Israel's last judge.

Making Connections

Last week, our community studied the story of Ruth and Naomi, who found strength in their relationship with each other. This week, Hannah and Peninnah are in a similar situation; two women, bonded by chosen family, one of whom grieves the loss or absence of a child. We know from last week's story that companionship lessens the burden of grief, and yet Peninnah chooses to worsen Hannah's burdens by taunting her. How might Hannah's story have been different if she had been able to find comfort, rather than pain, in her relationship with Peninnah?

Questions for Contemplation

1. Hannah turns to God in prayer in both good times and bad. What is a time when you turned to God in prayer to ask for something? When was the last time you prayed to God in thanksgiving?
2. Hannah is remembered as a woman of faith not because her prayer was answered, but because she remained faithful to God in both challenging and fulfilling seasons. What does it mean to you to be a woman of faith, even when you cannot see God's hand in your life in this minute?
3. Does Hannah's example change the way you think about prayer? If so, how?

Journaling Prompt:

In her prayer of thanksgiving, Hannah says that "here is none holy like the Lord: for there is none besides you; there is no rock like our God" (1 Samuel 2:2). This language reminds me of the verse and often-repeated phrase, "my rock and my redeemer." For today's journaling entry, we will focus on the imagery of God as rock and redeemer. How is God a "rock" in your life? You may wish to illustrate a mountain, a boulder, or an assurance-giving pebble in your pocket. Or you may wish to letter Hannah's words however you wish. Whatever approach you take, let the words and imagery of Hannah's story guide you as you journal today.

13

MARY

This week's reading: Luke 1:26-56, John 2:1-11, John 19:25

This week's journaling focus: Luke 1:28-30

Few women are as remembered and revered as Mary, mother of Jesus. Some traditions see her as an intercessor; others, as an inspiring example of heart and humility. Though the popularity of a name can't tell us of the importance of its namesake, the fact that Mary in all its forms — Maria, Marilyn, Marie, and others — is one of the most popular names in the Western world, should tell us something about just what a grip Mary of Nazareth has on our culture. And of course this is the case, because Mary is not just known for who she was, but for who she brought into the world: Jesus, the way, the truth, and the light. In being his mother, Mary experienced love, joy, pain, and devastation, and earned herself a place in history. All this from a young girl living in an ordinary town, who just happened to be favored by an extraordinary God.

Join and journal with us as we study Mary, mother of Jesus.

Mary's Story

Part One: Visitation

In the region of Galilee is a small town called Nazareth; so small and inconsequential that in John 1:46, Nathanael says of it, "Can anything good come out of [there]?" In this town lives a young girl named Mary, engaged to a man named Joseph. Many have tried to estimate Mary's age, and ideas have ranged anywhere from 13 to 19, but 15 is a popular guess.

As a teenage girl living in a small community in Galilee, Mary probably did not have high aspirations for herself or her life. But that understanding changes with one visit, when the angel Gabriel comes to Mary one day and said,

"Greetings, O favored one, the Lord is with you!"
Luke 1:28

Mary is troubled by this, but the angel tells her not

to be afraid, "for you have found favor with God" (Luke 1:30). Next, he says words that would likely terrify and overwhelm most of us:

"And behold, you will conceive in your womb and bear a son, and you shall call his name Jesus. He will be great and will be called the Son of the Most High. And the Lord God will give to him the throne of his father David, and he will reign over the house of Jacob forever, and of his kingdom there will be no end."

Luke 1:31-33

But Mary's response doesn't indicate that she is overwhelmed or afraid. Instead, she just seems perplexed, asking, "How will this be, since I am a virgin?" (Luke 1:34). Gabriel explains that "The Holy Spirit will come upon you, and the power of the Most High will overshadow you; therefore the child to be born will be called holy—the Son of God" (Luke 1:35). He explains that her cousin, Elizabeth, is also pregnant despite her old age, adding "For nothing is impossible with the Lord" (Luke 1:38). Those of us who remember Sarah's story may smile at these words.

Mary's response may surprise some of us. We might expect her to have more questions; to protest, like Moses did, when God interrupts life with His plans. But Mary doesn't ask. She doesn't protest. She doesn't turn the angel away. Instead, she accepts, saying,

"Behold, I am the servant of the Lord; let it be to me according to your word."

Luke 1:38

And the angel leaves her.

Despite Mary's humility and acceptance of her fate, however, she is still a young girl in a difficult situation.

80

There are many parts of her story that might be troubling to her. Perhaps Joseph will leave her, or the people of Nazareth will judge her, making assumptions that aren't true. At around only fifteen, she is still young and inexperienced, and likely knew very little about pregnancy. So Mary turns to someone who she knew could help her: her cousin Elizabeth. When Mary greets Elizabeth, Elizabeth's baby leaps in her womb, and she cries,

"Blessed are you among women, and blessed is the fruit of your womb! And why is this granted to me that the mother of my Lord should come to me?"

Luke 1:42-43

This is how Elizabeth becomes the first person to recognize Jesus. We will explore her story next week. Today, we focus on Mary's response, a song which has been put to music for centuries.

"My soul magnifies the Lord, and my spirit rejoices in God my Savior, for he has looked on the humble estate of his servant. For behold, from now on all generations will call me blessed; for he who is mighty has done great things for me, and holy is his name. And his mercy is for those who fear him from generation to generation. He has shown strength with his arm; he has scattered the proud in the thoughts of their hearts; he has brought down the mighty from their thrones and exalted those of humble estate; he has filled the hungry with good things, and the rich he has sent away empty. He has helped his servant Israel, in remembrance of his mercy, as he spoke to our fathers, to Abraham and to his offspring forever."

Luke 1:46-55

Mary weaves together verses and structures from the Old Testament scriptures, using them to proclaim her son's and her own place in the telling of God's story.

Part Two: Departing

Not much is known of Jesus' childhood, but in what we do hear of it, from his birth, his presentation in the Temple, and the early flight to Egypt, Mary is always there. In Jesus' ministries, she is sometimes mentioned, either as being there or being honored by members of the crowd. But we don't truly meet and hear from Mary again until John 19, at the scene of Christ's crucifixion:

"Standing by the cross of Jesus were his mother and his mother's sister, Mary the wife of Clopas, and Mary Magdalene. When Jesus saw his mother and the disciple whom he loved standing nearby, he said to his mother, "Woman, behold, your son!" Then he said to the disciple, "Behold, your mother!" And from that hour the disciple took her to his own home."

John 19:25-27

Mary's pain standing at the foot of the cross is unimaginable. When we focus on Mary, we often focus on the early parts of her story: the joy and overwhelm at bearing the Son of God. But we shouldn't forget this portion of her life. Though it is marked by grief and pain, this is the chapter of her life in which her role in God's story is fulfilled. The pain we feel at Jesus' crucifixion is changed when we remember that it is the very story that gives us life and freedom.

Mary witnesses, first-hand, the fulfillment of God's promise. She brings Jesus into the world and witnesses him being taken from it. And we, with her, are ushered into the blessing that the fulfillment of that promise brings.

Making Connections

Time and time again in this study, we have encountered women who waited for many years to have children. Often, the delay that led up to a child coming into the world only served to show the importance of that child in the story of God: Isaac, Jacob, and Samuel are examples of this. But Mary's story defies that convention. She was not married, like Rachel or Hannah; she did not pray for children, like Sarah did, or receive a child in her old age, like Elizabeth. She was young, unwed, and a virgin. And God used that very part of her story to usher into the world the most important figure in God's story: Jesus of Nazareth. In light of the many stories about motherhood we've seen, how does Mary's story stand out? Does this show us anything important about who Mary was, or why God might have chosen her?

Questions for Contemplation

1. Unlike other mothers in the Women of Valor series, Mary did not want or pray for a child. Still, God chose her to be the mother of Jesus. What about Mary or her heart may have made her the right choice to be the mother of Jesus?

2. Mary has been remembered and honored for generations by people of all backgrounds and denominations. Do you think this is because of her appointment as the mother of Jesus, or also because of her own character? What about Mary makes her stand out to you?

Journaling Prompt:

Today we examined two parts of Mary's story. The first was the visitation of the angel to Mary, when Mary first finds out that she will be the bearer of God's son. You may choose to illustrate this exchange, showing Gabriel and Mary or lettering the words from their exchange that stand out to you. Or you may choose to journal the latter part of Mary's story, when she witnesses her son on the cross, drawing the moment or lettering the words "Woman, behold your son." Whichever story strikes you, let that inspiration guide you as you journal in your Bible today.

14

ELIZABETH

This week's reading: Luke 1:5-80

This week's journaling focus: Luke 1:41-43

In my first year of college, I attended an Advent worship service that focused on the relationship between Mary and Elizabeth. Through scripture and stories, we read about how Elizabeth served as a mentor and friend for Mary, and our worship leader encouraged this group of young women to look for the "Elizabeths" in our own lives.

That lesson has stuck with me for years, and now, every time I read the story of Elizabeth, I can't help but think of her and Mary together, and the special bond between them. Though Elizabeth and Mary were pregnant at the same time, they were in very different situations. Mary was young, unmarried, and had not asked or prayed for a child before being blessed with one by the Holy Spirit. Elizabeth was "advanced in years" (Luke 1:7) and had long been barren; and, like many of the women in our study, had longed for a child for decades. But those differences must have been a blessing to both of them in their time together, as Elizabeth could guide and mentor Mary through her pregnancy, and Mary undoubtedly brought joy to Elizabeth's life. We can only imagine the friendship that blossomed between them in their months together; a friendship that would live on between their sons, John the Baptist and Jesus.

Join us as we journal the story of Elizabeth.

Elizabeth's Story

Part One: Waiting

In the days of Herod lived a man, Zechariah, and his wife Elizabeth. They were "righteous," living "blamelessly in all the commandments and statutes of the Lord" (Luke 1:6). Elizabeth was barren. Those of us who have been participating in the Women of Valor study are likely very familiar with this story by now, thanks to the stories of women like Sarah and Hannah. We know from their stories that the children who came from those unlikely pregnancies would go on to be a blessing to the people of Israel. Elizabeth's story is no exception, as we will soon see.

Zechariah is a priest, and eventually it becomes his turn to enter the temple of the Lord to burn incense. This happened about once in a lifetime, and was surely a very meaningful moment for a man who had spent his life following the commandments of God. But Zechariah had no idea just how meaningful this day would be to him, until he was approached by the angel Gabriel, who said,

"Do not be afraid, Zechariah, for your prayer has been heard, and your wife Elizabeth will bear you a son, and you shall call his name John. And you will have joy and gladness, and many will rejoice at his birth, for he will be great before the Lord. And he must not drink wine or strong drink, and he will be filled with the Holy Spirit, even from his mother's womb. And he will turn many of the children of Israel to the Lord their God, and he will go before him in the spirit and power of Elijah, to turn the hearts of the fathers to the children, and the disobedient to the wisdom of the just, to make ready for the Lord a people prepared."

1 Luke 13-18

Zechariah doubts the angel's words, and in punishment, Gabriel takes away his ability to speak until the birth of his son. Elizabeth does become pregnant, and in that time, Mary receives her own visitation from Gabriel.

Part Two: Receiving

Mary goes to visit her relative Elizabeth in the hill country, traveling for many weeks to see her. When Elizabeth and Mary first lay eyes on each other, Elizabeth experiences something extraordinary: "the baby leaped in her womb. And Elizabeth was filled with the Holy Spirit" (Luke 1:41). She cries,

"Blessed are you among women, and blessed is the fruit of your womb! And why is this granted to me that the mother of my Lord should come to me? For behold, when the sound of your greeting came to my ears, the baby in my womb leaped for joy. And blessed is she who believed that there would be a fulfillment of what was spoken to her from the Lord."

Luke 1:42-45

And so, Elizabeth becomes the first person to identify Jesus as Lord. Mary responds with her Magnificat, which we read last week. Many have put Mary's words to music, but few remember the words of Elizabeth, which are also beautiful: "And blessed is she who believed that there would be a fulfillment of what was spoken to her from the Lord" (Luke 1:45). Though Zechariah had doubted the angel Gabriel's words, Mary and Elizabeth both believe. Blessed are they.

Elizabeth and Mary stay together for many months, until it is time for them to give birth. When Elizabeth's baby is born, and on the day that he is to be circumcised, Zechariah names him John. He regains the ability to speak, and immediately blesses the Lord. "And the child grew and became strong in spirit," the text tells us. He becomes John the Baptist, who baptized and walked alongside Jesus.

Making Connections

We have now read three stories about an older woman who prayed to have a child: Sarah, Hannah, and Elizabeth. In each case, she ultimately went on to bear a child who would be important to the future of Israel: Isaac, Samuel, and John the Baptist.

However, not all of us find or receive our gifts through children. Sometimes, the dreams that we wait on can take on a different meaning. Perhaps a life goal of a different kind - a job, a home, a skill - comes at another time than you expected or hoped for, on God's timeline and not your own. Will you laugh, like Sarah? Pray, like Hannah? Accept, like Elizabeth? Perhaps all three. Or perhaps you will find comfort in their stories, in which a dream deferred often means a dream fulfilled, better or more deeply than it would have been before.

Questions for Contemplation

1. Mary and Elizabeth stayed together for many months. We can only imagine the joy and comfort that they found in each other, both blessed by extraordinary and unexpected pregnancies at a time in their lives where it was not what they had expected or maybe even wanted. How do you find comfort in the women in your life in times of trouble?

2. Are there anyone in your life who could benefit from a mentor like Elizabeth? How might you be a blessing to them?

Journaling Prompt:

Today we will focus on the last of the words that Elizabeth spoke upon seeing Mary: "And blessed is she who believed that there would be a fulfillment of what was spoken to her from the Lord" (Luke 1:45). Where has God fulfilled his words to you in your life? You may want to illustrate that with sketches, painting, or photos. Or you may wish to illustrate Mary and Elizabeth together, bonding over the differences and similarities between them. Finally, you may wish to letter the words in a way that feels right to you. Let the Holy Spirit guide you in your journaling practice today!

15

MARY MAGDALENE

This week's reading: Luke 8:1-3, Mark 15:40, Mark 27:56, Mark 15:47, Matthew 27:61, Matthew 28:1, Mark 16:1, John 20:1-18

This week's journaling focus: John 20:18

Of all the women in the New Testament, Mary Magdalene may have the worst reputation — and the least-deserved! Many people believe that Mary Magdalene, who was one of the female followers and companions of Jesus, was a prostitute; however, there is no Biblical reference to this (the belief probably came from the fact that the first mention of her follows the story of a sinful woman). All we know about Mary Magdalene, or Mary of Magdala, is that she was an afflicted woman, possessed by seven demons before Jesus healed her. After her encounter with Jesus, Mary Magdalene spent her life following Jesus, and became one of the best-remembered and most-revered women of the Bible. She is listed in every gospel, is the first woman named to follow Jesus, and is the first person to witness the Resurrection. Join us today as we journal the story of Mary Magdalene, who walked with Christ.

Mary Magdalene's Story

Part One: Encountering Jesus

We don't know very much about Mary Magdalene first-hand. Instead, we hear a few facts about her life in retrospective and are left to fill in the blanks. The first we hear of her is in Luke 8:1, when Jesus is traveling through the cities and villages, "proclaiming and bringing the good news of the kingdom of God" (Luke 8:1). With him are the disciples and "some women who had been healed of evil spirits and infirmities," including "Mary, called Magdalene, from whom seven demons had gone out" (Luke 8:2).

Along with the other two women who are said to follow Jesus in this verse, Joanna and Susanna, Mary is said to "provided for them out of their means," indicating that she might have come from some wealth and status. This is certainly possible — Mary is called the Magdalene because she came from a coastal town called Magdala, which was known to be wealthy through dyes and textiles. It is possible that Mary's family benefitted from these trades, and that these were the means that she was able to pour into Jesus' work and ministry. What we know of Mary's past, then, is that she was a woman who struggled with illness and evil until she encountered Jesus, and that after he healed her, she spent her life following him.

Part Two: At the Cross and Tomb

The next we hear of Mary Magdalene is at the time of the death of Jesus in Mark 15. Jesus has been convicted, mocked and belittled, and crucified. At the time of his last breath, the centurion watching the crucifixion says, "Truly this man was the Son of God!" (Mark 15:39). We read that the women watch from afar, Mary Magdalene among them. The pain and anguish that these women must have felt is unbelievable. They likely believed that this was the 'end' of the story; but as we know, it is only the beginning.

After Jesus is wrapped in linen and brought to the tomb, Mary Magdalene and another Mary see where Jesus was laid and sit opposite the tomb (Mark 15:47, Matthew 27:61). The following morning, they go to the tomb to anoint him with spices when they find the tomb empty (Matthew 28:1, Mark 16:1, John 20:1). When they see the stone was rolled away, Mary runs to Simon Peter and "the other disciple" and cries, "They have taken the Lord out of the tomb, and we do not know where they have laid him." (John 20:2). The disciples, not understanding that Jesus would rise again, returned to their homes; but Mary stayed, weeping, and Jesus appeared to her (John 20:8-14):

Jesus said to her, "Woman, why are you weeping? Whom are you seeking?" Supposing him to be the gardener, she said to him, "Sir, if you have carried him away, tell me where you have laid him,

and I will take him away." Jesus said to her, "Mary." She turned
and said to him in Aramaic, "Rabboni!" (which means
Teacher). Jesus said to her, "Do not cling to me, for I have not yet
ascended to the Father; but go to my brothers and say to them, 'I am
ascending to my Father and your Father, to my God and your God.'"

John 20:15-17

Mary listened, running to the disciples. And she told them, "I have seen the Lord," and repeated his words to her.

Making Connections
Though there were several women who followed Jesus and participated in his ministry, Mary Magdalene is the best-known, likely because she was the first named and the first person to whom Jesus appeared after the Resurrection. Like Mary of Nazareth and Elizabeth, who we have studied in previous weeks, Mary Magdalene recognized the divinity of Jesus. Unlike those two women, she came from a place of immense darkness, and then devoted her life to following Jesus, literally walking beside him as he journeyed from city to city. How is Mary Magdalene's story a metaphor for our own journeys with God?

Questions for Contemplation
1. Mary Magdalene was afflicted with seven demons before Jesus healed her. After Jesus came into her life, Mary Magdalene was healed and followed him, and though we know that her life was not perfect or pain-free even after meeting Christ, we know that

94

she found fulfillment and a lifelong journey in walking beside Jesus. Do you identify with Mary Magdalene's transition from a place of darkness to one of light? Is there another part of her story that you identify with?

2. How do the themes of Mary Magdalene's story, such as redemption or discipleship, play out in your own life?

Journaling Prompt:

Mary Magdalene's story is a beautiful example of a life walked with Jesus. Mary was plagued by demons until she was healed through an encounter with Jesus, and following that encounter, she spent her life following him. Her life was not "perfect" after first meeting Jesus; she still experienced pain and suffering of her own, as we are reminded when she witnesses the crucifixion from afar. But Mary finds joy again, when Jesus appears to her after his resurrection. She breathlessly runs to the disciples and says to them, "I have seen the Lord." Focus on these words as you journal today. You may want to illustrate Mary seeing Jesus after he has risen, or illustrate your own "encounters" with Jesus throughout your life. Or you may choose to letter the words, focusing on what they mean to you.

16

PHOEBE

This week's reading: Romans 16:1-2

This week's journaling focus: Romans 16:1-2

It may seem strange to end a study of women of the Bible with Phoebe. We have studied Sarah, Miriam, and Mary — women who appear across chapters and books — and skipped over women like Eve and Deborah, who certainly play a large role in the narrative arc of the

Bible. Phoebe, on the other hand, is only mentioned in a single sentence, in the Book of Romans. But through that sentence, we receive hints of a life dedicated to the church and its people, and we are inspired by an example of generosity and dedication. Today, we study and journal Phoebe as a means of looking back across the women of this study, and looking into our own lives.

Phoebe's Story

Part One: A Life of Service

Paul mentions Phoebe at the end of his letter to the Romans, as she is the person who delivered his letter to Rome. He writes,

> *I commend to you our sister Phoebe, a servant of the church at Cenchreae, that you may welcome her in the Lord in a way worthy of the saints, and help her in whatever she may need from you, for she has been a patron of many and of myself as well.*
> Romans 16:1-2

From this short description of Phoebe, we can learn a few things about her life. First, we know that she was a servant of the church, though the word "servant" here has been debated by many scholars. A more accurate translation may be "deacon," meaning that Phoebe would have had a position of authority in her worship community. Whether or not that was the case, we know from Paul's description of her and from her willingness to make the journey to Rome, that Phoebe was deeply devoted to the work of the church. For a woman, this was quite an honor and a rarity at that time.

We can also tell from Paul's description of Phoebe that he feels deeply grateful to her for the work that she has done. He calls for the Romans to treat her "in a way worthy of the saints" and "help her in whatever way she may need" because she has been a patron for many, including Paul himself. Phoebe's generosity, then, is both in terms of her time, and in terms of her gifts. Like Mary Magdalene from last week, Phoebe was likely born into wealth and used her gifts to serve the church and maintain its servants. She also used her spiritual and earthy gifts — time, patience, and the freedom to travel — to serve the church in bringing Paul's letter to the Romans.

Part Two: A Legacy of Inspiration

For the final week of our study, we are studying Phoebe because the brevity and openness of her story allows us to look into our own lives. We know next to nothing about Phoebe's life: her marital status, potential children, work, finances, dwelling, or anything else. We know next to nothing about her character: whether she was kind, or serious, or gentle, or loud. But we know that, whoever she was, she used her gifts to serve her community and the worldwide church.

Today, the church encompasses many traditions and beliefs, from Orthodoxy to Catholicism to Protestantism and beyond. Sometimes, we may feel that those traditions and beliefs divide, rather than unite us. But wherever we may fall in the 'family tree' of the Christian faith, we all share a common heart: a desire to know Jesus and the life he lived, and to live like him in the world. His example of service and sacrifice should inspire each of us, as it clearly inspired Phoebe.

In the Women of Valor study, we have up to now

learned the stories of eleven women: Hagar, Sarah, Rebecca, Leah, Rachel, Miriam, Ruth, Hannah, Mary, Elizabeth, and Mary Magdalene. Though themes and symbols may sometimes echo throughout multiple stories, each woman's story is different, demonstrating different strengths and weaknesses of character. Not so for Phoebe, whose life and character we know very little of. Instead, her example of generosity and service allows us to look into ourselves and see how we may or may not be using our own gifts to better and bless the lives of others.

Making Connections

Throughout this study, we have seen several women who used their gifts of character or means to contribute to the world. Miriam, for example, was a prophetess who led her people, and Mary Magdalene used her earthly gifts to help fund and support the church. Phoebe seems to have given both spiritual and earthly gifts, in a true example of generosity. Her example of service allows us to look at our own lives, seeing where our own qualities may be being used to help others or contribute to the church.

Questions for Contemplation

1. Take a quick look through the pages of your journaling Bible, stopping on the pages that correlate to our Women of Valor study. Reflect on these women and their stories. Many of them have strong characteristics, such as stubbornness, faithfulness, or humility. Which qualities, good and bad, do you recognize within yourself?

2. Next, think about the different spiritual gifts that these women had. Some had a special gift for prayer,

such as Hannah; for supporting a friend like Elizabeth did; or for leading others, as did Miriam. Which gifts have others pointed out in you? Are there any that you see in yourself?

3. Finally, think about these gifts in the broader context of the world. You were given your exact combination of strengths, weaknesses, and qualities with purpose; because there is something about your place in the world, or lives that you will touch, that benefits from these qualities. How could you use them to serve like Phoebe did? Try not to limit yourself to practical ideas, like strictly donating money or time. Is there a skill you have that would help you mentor someone, or that you could use to raise money in a special way? Is there a quality or characteristic you have that makes you an especially good friend or parent? What is something about you that could be a gift to others?

Journaling Prompt:

Today's journaling entry is unique because we are not journaling a story, but instead, a theme. You (yes, you!) have gifts and talents that were given to you just as they were to Phoebe and the many other women we have encountered in this journaling study. In today's entry, journal as a way of expressing whatever gifts and talents you see in yourself and offering then up to God. Maybe you have a listening ear, and want to journal yourself listening to a child, or you listening to God's voice in your life. Maybe you have a talent for crafting or baking, and want to journal about that as a means of saying thank you to God for the gifts He has given you. Or maybe you struggle to see your own best qualities, but know that God has given you the gift of His love and grace, and just want to express your gratitude for that. However you decide to journal the message of Phoebe's generosity today, try not to let yourself get hung up on "shoulds" or "coulds." You've made it through twelve weeks of this study - you really can do this!

17

CONCLUSION

Congratulations on completing the Women of Valor study! As we have journeyed and journaled with the twelve women in this study, we have seen countless different examples of what it means to be a woman of valor. And time and time again, we have witnessed not only the skills and weaknesses of these women, but also the grace and mercy shown to them by an extraordinary God.

When we read the stories of these matriarchs and heroines, we may feel insignificant by comparison. But in doing so, we forget that each of these women would likely have called herself completely ordinary. In the eyes of the world, many of them were forgotten or overlooked: Hagar was a slave; Ruth was a foreigner and a convert; Mary was an unmarried teenager. They most likely knew and disliked their own flaws: Sarah was untrusting, Rebecca was deceitful, and Rachel was bitter. But God did not forget or overlook them. He used their traits for good, allowing each of these women to play an important role in the unfolding of these stories.

You are no different from these women: maybe overlooked by the world, maybe flawed in your own eyes, but seen and cherished by a merciful and loving God. The same God who saw Hagar; who kept His promises to Sarah; who trusted Rebecca; who brought love to Leah and Rachel; who gave Miriam the gift of leadership; who protected Ruth; who heard Hannah; who chose Mary; who blessed Elizabeth; who walked alongside Mary Magdalene;

and who guided Phoebe in building up the church. You are a part of the tapestry, another shimmering thread contributing to the richness and complexity of our story. His story.

ABOUT THE AUTHOR

Sara Laughed is a writer, blogger, and student of Religion. After beginning Bible journaling just before her confirmation, she began writing journaling studies in the fall of 2015 with *Advent Illustrated: Journey Through the Bible*, which saw 2,000 people creatively journal through the Advent season together. Since then, her studies have been read and journaled all over the world.

Sara most enjoys learning and spending time with loved ones. She is immensely grateful for the opportunity to study with you, and wishes you a meaningful and inspiring time journaling with the Women of the Bible.

RESOURCES AND LINKS

This study includes access to a variety of extra resources and downloads.

There are free downloads, including weekly printables for each of the women in this study, on our site Seasons Illustrated. You can access the Printable Library at http://seasonsillustrated.com/free-library using the password: psalm16:8

Our Facebook group is a great community to keep you inspired. Join us by searching for "Seasons Illustrated" on Facebook or by going to https://www.facebook.com/groups/seasonsillustrated/

You can also follow us on social media for updates:

Facebook: /seasonsillustrated
Instagram: @seasonsillustrated
Twitter: @seasillustrated
Pinterest: @seasillustrated

#seasonsillustrated

Made in the USA
Lexington, KY
01 May 2018